100 Ways

TO LIVE A

Soft, Calm Life

D1714798

FIONA FERRIS

Contents

100 Ways to Live a Soft, Calm Life........................... 7

50 Ways to Romanticize Your Everyday 73

To Finish.. 93

About the Author.. 97

Other books by Fiona Ferris................................. 99

Dear lovely reader,

In our world of looming deadlines, fast-paced news, and the ever-present daily hustle of work, laundry and coming up with three meals a day, it's easy to feel pressured and harried.

Even I feel it, and I am speaking as someone who doesn't have children and now works from home, and has a wonderfully supportive husband too. For many of us it's an external thing, but it can also be internal as well.

We feel the need to measure up, to be the perfect wife, sister, partner, mother, friend or daughter. We berate ourselves if we eat, drink, or spend too much. We judge ourselves on being too loud, too talkative, or not as perfect as others we see. It's exhausting, as I'm sure you can relate!

Over the years I have enjoyed learning how to nurture my femininity. Before that I didn't really think about the masculine or feminine side of me, I was just who I was. But I found out I was actually living a lot in my masculine, by being constantly on the go, creating stressful deadlines, and then becoming highly annoyed with myself when I fell short.

I would lean towards the feminine with my love of beauty products and taking time to cleanse and moisturise my skin at night. I dressed in colourful clothing that made me feel happy, and I read romantic and cozy novels.

But all this felt a bit frivolous and not what the real world was made of. They were almost like my guilty pleasures that I should hide to myself.

Now I know differently. I know that we ignore our feminine desires at our peril. It can be bad for our relationships, draining on our delicate nervous system, and just less fun too.

I can still feel like it's a waste of time to rest with a book for half an hour – *I'll read later when I've finished all my jobs*. But then the day runs out and I haven't read at all, squeezing in five minutes before I go to sleep.

If you too are an on-the-go woman and don't often give yourself time for creative pursuits, relaxation, or pretty, feminine, gentle things, I think you will love this book, and hopefully gain validation from it too. *Validation that you are someone who deserves to live a soft, calm, peaceful and serene life.*

There is no price to pay, and no-one will be hurt or inconvenienced. There really is no downside. It's not something that has to take a lot of time or even be noticeable to others. All they will see is that you are enjoying life more, looking more radiant, happier, and incredibly you might even get more done than you already do. That's what I have found in my own experience. I am more productive, yet happier and more relaxed than when I put myself last and try to 'do all my jobs first'.

And your health might improve too. I know that holding onto stress by worrying about 'whatever' (nothing important usually!) gives me a furrow between my eyebrows and causes my shoulders to feel tight and sore.

This is why it is so important to remind and reinspire yourself that *it's okay* to lean back into your feminine self. When you live in a softer state more often than not, you will feel perpetually relaxed and calm, your muscles will feel soft and fluid – almost like you're filled with gel.

And when you do lose your cool, you will come back to your equilibrium pretty quickly, and you will probably be grumpy less often too. At least that's what I have found for myself. It's such a lovely feeling, and I hope that by the end of this book you will feel the same!

With all my best from my cozy home office in beautiful Hawke's Bay, New Zealand,

100 Ways to Live
a Soft, Calm Life

1. **Take a moment to dream about this kind of life**. How would it look? How would it feel? What kinds of things would you do? When I think about living a soft, calm life, it feels cozy and feminine. I'd indulge in gentle body movement, take petite pleasures daily, and cultivate an overall aura of contentment and happiness. I'd focus on letting life be gentler and easier. I would feel compassion but try not to take on the stress of the world. I would look for ways to simplify my surroundings and my schedule. I'd make time to do more of the things I enjoy such as sewing, reading, and pottering. Why not design *your* ideal experience by making notes of everything

that would feel peaceful, relaxing, and restorative to you. Write down the details. Gaze at this beautiful life that is waiting for you and choose one or two things to do today. For me, I will enjoy a stretching session after my shower, and finish off a sewing project. What about you?

2. **Don't try to change anyone else**. You are doing this for you. You are reading this book and inspiring yourself to live a softer life. You don't need to force anyone else to do the same. But by *your* changing, they may also feel like they want to upgrade things. You will create a ripple effect with your renewed energy. Isn't it great that all you have to focus on is yourself? No extra effort to control others required? I learned this eventually, and letting go of the reins feels so good now. It's like you've given up the struggle and are gliding effortlessly along. Work on yourself, and find out what *you* enjoy. Brainstorm happiness lists in your journal. You will soon start to find that others are attracted to you, and may even start to change how they do things too. Just remind yourself: everything you are practicing, you are doing for yourself.

3. **Float in love**. When my dad died in 2018, I had this vision of his soul floating in love. It just came to me, and it was the most beautiful,

peaceful feeling I've ever felt. Even though I miss him every day and still wish he was here, I now feel okay about where he is. He is no longer an age or a physical body. He no longer feels any pain like we mere humans do. He is embodied as love on the non-physical plane. I have often thought about that day when this feeling was shown to me, and it helps me feel more at peace in my own life too. I let myself float in love when I need to, and it feels wonderful. I invite you to try this as well. Do it anytime you need a little calm. Imagine your inner self being weightless, supported, and surrounded by a deep, secure sense of love. It's like the best, warmest bath you have ever taken.

4. **Let your life be easy**. Accept help from others when it's offered. Ask for help from those in your household. Drop the martyr act; no-one likes it, least of all you! Find ways to simplify tasks you need to do. Stop and think before you end up with more responsibilities, pets, possessions or anything else that will require more time to take care of. Ask yourself when something is weighing you down, 'How can I make this easier?' Sometimes you will find you don't need to do that job at all, or you can streamline it. I used to note our daily household spending on a spreadsheet and thought it was necessary to keep on top of our

financial life. When we moved house I missed a month and found it hard to catch up, and ever after that I always felt behind. One day I just decided not to do that spreadsheet anymore and several years later I don't miss it. Anything I need to look up is on our bank's website. The rare time I do need to look up a purchase it might take a little longer, but because I don't spend time every week updating my spreadsheet, I am definitely winning. What can you let go of?

5. **Lower your expectations of other people**. Anytime I have been sorely disappointed by the actions of anyone, it's because I was expecting them to approach the situation as I would. And why should they? They didn't get my memo! I have now adopted a different outlook. I have low expectations of others, and high expectations of myself. I know this might sound unkind, but it's not meant that way. It just means I don't have this invisible sky-high standard for other people. That way, I don't end up disappointed. And, I get to focus on my own standards, which are the only ones I *can* control.

6. **Adopt a daily standard of appearance** that is appropriate for your lifestyle and easy to maintain. I love watching Hallmark-type movies. There is something so comforting

about their happy-ever-after small-town stories, and I especially love that the heroine is always well turned out. She is never in bombshell glam outfits, just pretty, feminine normal clothes. These movies are actually really good inspiration for everyday wear. And, the main character always has nice hair and makeup, jewellery and accessories. No matter what you are doing or wearing, spend five minutes on your grooming. It's wonderful to feel polished and always-ready with your Hallmark-style 'dressy but casual' look.

7. **Foster a deep appreciation for your home** and everyday life. Our home is the place that soothes and encloses us. We return there every day and are refreshed for the next. We get to be surrounded by our comforts and favourite things. We play, rest, and relax there. Sometimes we can take our home for granted though, I know I can. But when I remember how lucky I am, it's like a gift all over again. I am at a different stage in life now and live in a nice home that is fully paid off, but I remember feeling that same sense of wellbeing when I was renting a room in a house with three other girls. My bedroom was my haven and I appreciated it so much. I kept it nice and slept well at night. No matter your living situation, there will be many things you can be grateful for.

8. **Prioritize little treats for yourself**. It's good to be intentional with how you spend your time and money, as well as focusing on your values when you do so. My values include creativity, peace, and feeling cozy. I am a thrifty girl, and have always been careful with money, so for me it's actually been a practice to buy a few things for myself that I might not have in the past. These include a Starbucks special coffee, a new candle, a pretty jigsaw, or a paperback book that appeals. What purchases would be joyful and could you work them into your budget every now and then?

9. **Have daily quiet time**. Just as children might have quiet time at school or home to calm their busy, over-stimulated minds, why not take this concept on for yourself? You could choose to take a walk outside without listening to anything, read a real turn-the-page book, work on a jigsaw puzzle, or journal with pen and paper. Whatever you do, it wouldn't involve a screen or anything verbal such as a podcast or television show. It might be hard to do at the start, it was for me, but I decided to have at least thirty minutes of quiet time each day to counteract my mind ping-ponging everywhere. Set a timer to begin with to prevent you from rushing off to do something that you've just thought of. In our busy lives with a million distractions this is the reality for

many of us. The fact that it is hard to do is the wake-up call to say that *we need our daily quiet time*. This is something you can start today. Claim it for yourself.

10. **Get your life in order**. As you tidy up your home, declutter excess belongings, use up items you habitually over-purchase, get your financial admin under control, clean your fridge, simplify your schedule and identify loose ends (and complete them), you will begin to feel calmer. It's a gloriously addictive feeling. Make it a little goal each day to do *something* towards getting your life in order. Practice habits such as cleaning your kitchen counter before you go to bed, and making your bed first thing in the morning so these things become what you do automatically. When you keep an orderly, tidy life, it is far easier to feel calm and composed. Your clothes for the next day are clean, in good repair and hanging in the closet waiting for you. There is no last-minute scramble. Not every day will be perfect and you'll probably still forget a few things which means a bit of last-minute stress, I certainly do. But for the most part, you can feel good. It's a worthwhile goal, to get – and keep – your life in order.

11. **Make grocery shopping more enjoyable**. We all have to go to the supermarket each

week, and even if we get our groceries delivered, there are likely a few items which still need to be picked up. Instead of grocery shopping being a boring, begrudging chore, I have found a few ways to make it more enjoyable. Firstly, before I even leave the house, I like to be dressed in a cute but comfortable outfit. I put my hair up in a pretty ponytail so I can feel efficient. I have an audiobook or my favourite music cued up and ready to play on the way. My car is clean and empty, and I have a little purse with parking coins in it so I'm never stuck. Plus my bins and bags for bringing my groceries home. I always keep a bottle of water in my car, but a barista coffee when I am out is my little treat each week. Think about what stresses (or bores) you about grocery shopping, and upgrade your experience so you can enjoy it more.

12. **Have your own little secret garden doings**. I love the sparkly, happy feel-good time of Christmas, so at any time of the year I might play Christmas music when it's just me at home, or read a Christmas themed novel. I'll diffuse my Christmas-scented essential oils or light a Christmas candle. If I'm in the mood and it makes me happy, why not? It doesn't matter if it's July! Anyway, here in New Zealand we have our winter in the middle of the year, and holding a mid-year Christmas is

actually a thing. But regardless of the weather and how cold it is outside, I just like to sprinkle a little Christmas magic over an ordinary day when I'm in the mood. What happiness can you delight in just for yourself?

13. **Prepare a day of rest** and prioritize self-care. That way you can be productive and 'on' the rest of the time, and when you rest, you rest. 'Self-care Sunday' is a popular one, and Sundays in general are wonderful to 'do nothing'. You could choose to have no social media or work. Just read a book, watch a movie, and relax. Or you could designate Sunday to be a 'rest and reset' day where you put things in order for the following week. And while you're at it, why not throw in a few more times for rest during the week? Make Thursday nights the night where you apply a face mask and journal for a while. Or Saturday mornings where you go for a walk somewhere beautiful close by. Find these pockets in your schedule and book in restorative activities for yourself.

14. **Make everyday life an occasion**. Set up a little tray with your favourite hot drink, a sweet or savoury treat, and a book to carry outside. Bring a cozy rug too. Add small details into your day and make life feel more special. Create a life of comfort and luxury for yourself.

Gather petite pleasures and indulge in them often. Some of my favourites are going for a browse around the shops, making hot tea, watching vlogs or doing a yoga class at home (both on YouTube), tidying my bedroom and making it extra lovely, working on a sewing project, baking something using ingredients I have on hand (with a recipe I found online) and creating an everyday ambience in my home with lamps, candles, music, and diffused essential oils.

15. **Use all your senses**. Make your life 'sensational'. Go through the five senses and see if whatever you are doing touches them all: sight, sound, taste, smell, and touch. If you are doing something as perfunctory as cleaning out your closet, imagine doing so in a methodical fashion instead of throwing clothes everywhere. Have your favourite music playing softly, a cool, delicious bottle of water nearby, and a diffuser or candle scenting the room. You take the time to appreciate the textures as you sort, fold and hang. And you keep the vision in mind of how you want your personal style to evolve as you move forward. You'll find you can't help *but* be inspired when you bring all your senses into play.

16. **Appreciate and plan for seasonal treats**. Live seasonally by being in the season you are

in – spring, summer, winter, or autumn, and also look at special holidays such as Christmas, the summer and winter solstices, Valentines Day, or days that are personal to you. Make special meals, wear colours pertaining to the season, and take in seasonal entertainment too. I find doing this helps me be in the moment more which is always a welcome outcome. Approach each month or each quarter with a little plan, and a renewed sense of fun by immersing yourself in the current season.

17. **Approach fitness in a soft and gentle way**. There is no need to be all-or-nothing when it comes to fitness and aging well. I used to think that if I couldn't do 'proper gym workouts' (because I didn't want to!), then what was the point? But now I know better, and have devised a gentle fitness regime that I do most days. I have found that the less barriers to exercise there are, the more likely I am to keep the habit up. My yoga mat lives rolled up under the sideboard in our living room, and I use it every second day. Sometimes I'll just stretch, and sometimes I follow a yoga or Pilates class on YouTube. Starting is the hardest part, so 'just do it' and the rest will follow.

18. **Surround yourself with cozy textures**. Even if it's not cold outside it's still nice to drape a light throw over your legs while reading. Choose the softest cotton when you are buying tee-shirts. Pad around in bare feet on soft carpet or wear fuzzy socks if you have hardwood floors. Wear fine cotton palazzo pants or satin pyjama sets as lounge wear. Let everything that touches your skin feel good. In the past few years I have discovered pure linen sheets. Oh my gosh, they are lovely! I have built up our collection and almost have two complete sets – the final piece is another top sheet. They aren't cheap so I wait for special offers, and I know they will last us a while too.

19. **Read real books**. A wonderful way in which to live a calmer, softer life, is to look for ways to be more analogue. Choose paper over screens, do things in real life rather than sitting at a computer in your free time, and interact physically with others rather than via a text. Find handcrafts that appeal and start a new hobby. Invite your girlfriends around for afternoon tea, or go out for a walk whether it's around the city or through a park, and be face-to-face with people. Even at work you can choose to go and ask someone a question rather than email them. Or at home make cookies from scratch (it's quite easy!) instead of opening a packet. Just keep 'real life,

physical body, moving around' in mind and choose this whenever possible.

20. **Make the most of the calendar on your phone**. Most of us have a smartphone, and most smartphones come with a built-in calendar. Since I started using mine as the basis of my schedule, I have become more organized, and from this have been able to feel more relaxed since I didn't always have a nagging feeling that I've forgotten important things. You will have to remember to check it each day, but that will become a habit the more you do it. I still transfer appointments to a paper calendar in the kitchen and to the planner on my desk, but those are more for a quick glance. Making the phone calendar my main option means I don't double-book myself and my phone is always with me too so it's handy. At the hairdresser I make my next appointment while I'm there and it goes straight into my phone calendar. The great thing too is that you can put in recurring reminders for yourself – birthdays annually, and daily or weekly habits you are trying to put into place. I also have a small list of to-dos which I can delete once I've done them. You can access your calendar from different devices, and even print out that day, week or month if you want to.

21. **Choose to be an unruffled and less reactive person**. It's not that you are letting people get away with anything, it's just that you are choosing to live a more tranquil and settled daily life. Don't let others get under your skin. Practice being someone who lets slights – perceived or otherwise – slide away. Laugh it off and know that any harsh words say more about them than about you. As long as you know that what they are saying is untrue, you have nothing to worry about. And if there is a needling feeling that their words have some truth, you have something to work on. Honestly, we should *thank* the annoying people in our lives! The more I have worked on being an unbothered person, the happier and calmer I feel. And the times when I have *not* managed to keep my cool I feel horrible and it reminds me of my wish to be more laid back.

22. **Plan ahead to be relaxed**. As well as using the calendar on my phone as the first point of contact for my schedule, I also like to get ahead of the game by putting soft and gentle routines into place. I make sure I have fresh food in the fridge for the next few days of meals, and I prep a lunch for myself the day before even though I work from home. I put self-care and grooming into my calendar, so I remember to do them on certain days. I do laundry every day or two so that my clothes are always clean,

ironed and ready to wear. I don't plan out my outfits; it just feels better for me to have a seasonal selection to choose from. Keeping my home lightly tidy and clean is a form of planning ahead too. At different times when I've been tired or busy and any of these areas have fallen into disarray, it is reiterated to me that the small habits do matter. You don't have to be perfect, just do what needs to be done most of the time. You can let the odd day here and there slide; it actually feels quite nice to play hooky sometimes and then you will be energized and ready to pick up the pace again tomorrow!

23. **Book a facial four times a year**. It's never too early or too late in life to lavish more care and attention on your complexion. I love the idea of beginning each new season with a professional facial. It's a treat for you to look forward to, and it's also good for your skin as the seasons change. Every three months isn't too bad for the budget either. I've always wanted to have a regular facial, but once a month seemed too much. Quarterly is just perfect. And if quarterly is not in your budget, plan for a luxurious do-it-yourself facial at home – cleanse your face, exfoliate, and apply a mask. Treat it like your car service or medical checkup and plan for it - don't just think you'll

remember. I promise you from experience that you won't!

24. **Change your routines**. I love my deliciously restorative morning routine and I also love having a day off from it. Most days I'll rise at 6am and write for my books with a cup of hot tea, before doing a little exercise, walking the dogs, sipping my smoothie and taking a shower. And sometimes I'll do everything in the opposite order, or go completely free-range just because it feels good. Mostly I do my usual, but it feels nice to have the choice, don't you think? Whatever you routinely do, maybe switch it up. It will refresh your mind and make things seem new again, even if you're doing nothing particularly different.

25. **Take the opportunity to move slowly** when you can. On a day off at home, enjoy taking your time getting going in the morning. Sip tea, do tasks in a leisurely way, and tend to the details. If you are able to spend the whole day in this manner, you will find that not only have you got a lot done, but that you will feel utterly refreshed as well. Even if you have other family members around you including children, intentionally slow down your movements and your thoughts. Do one thing at a time and finish it before you move on. Clean up as you go. Fluff and tidy. Prep your

evening meal earlier in the day and I promise it will feel like someone else did all the work, not you!

26. **Switch your soft mindset on**. You can't just stomp around and wait for this mythical life of ease and beauty to fall over you like a cashmere cloak. Remind yourself to lean back into the goodness of your life and enjoy it if you don't often remember to do so. If you are too busy holding your physical self tensely, preparing for whatever the day might hold for you, let your poor hunched body relax, not be waiting for the next drama. Unwelcome situations big and small will always happen, but you don't need to anticipate them. Each day needs to be about you deciding to prioritize a soft mindset over everything else. It's about letting things be as they are and not getting wound up over petty happenings. Annoying situations can be dealt with in a calm manner. They are not personal. You don't need to become irritated and bothered that these things have happened. You can choose to be calm, at ease, and carefree (while still kicking butt!)

27. **Halve your sugar intake**. Something interesting I have noticed is that when I decide to 'treat myself' to something high in sugar, I am more easily irritated for the next day or so.

Plus I sleep really badly if I have eaten sweets after dinner. It is an irritant from the inside, not only that day but the next day too. It's still in our system. It's easier to sink into a soft, calm mindset when you limit your sugar. I call my way 'no sugar' but it's actually 'very little sugar'. So, instead of buying milk or white chocolate that is guaranteed to be eaten very quickly, I buy a minimum 70% cacao plain dark chocolate. It sounds boring, but two pieces after dinner with my coffee and I am sated. You don't need to cut out all sugar unless you want to, but perhaps you might choose a danger time to adjust what you consume like I did with the dark chocolate. You'll be grumpy at the time that you 'only' have dark chocolate available, but happy in the morning when you wake up bright and fresh, and not grumpy at all!

28.   **Keep a list of activities you'd love to spend a quiet half hour on**. The kinds of thing you wish you did more of, and that promote feelings of slowness, creativity and relaxation. I came up with this idea and created a list for myself which included such activities as reading a paper novel, browsing a glossy coffee table book, working a little on my current jigsaw, doing a guided meditation, dreaming up new outfit ideas in my closet, looking through my costume jewellery so I

don't forget to wear it, painting my nails, reading my style files, doing some journalling, or working on a small sewing project. It sounds a bit basic and silly, but if you're like me and always thinking you should be doing something on your to-do list, it's a real treat to indulge in one of the things on your to-play list.

29. **Show up in your life and be present**. If you are doing something, do it with a single focus and stay with it until it is complete. Perhaps it is a conversation with your husband or friend, or working on a task at home or work. Resisting the urge to multi-task or switch to another job that catches your eye will help you feel grounded. You're not asking your brain to dart around; it can work methodically and steadily. And when you are talking with someone, it is so easy to 'just check your phone'. *I know*, I feel it too. But put it in your bag, or another room if you're at home, and just *be there* with the person you are conversing with.

30. **Be *in* your body**. Do a ten-minute full body stretch, or a ten-minute sensual dance routine. Follow a video on YouTube for ideas. Move your body. Love your body. She wants to flow and sway, not be rigid like a dry twig. Set up a yoga mat permanently if you have the room or

at least have it rolled up nearby so you can have five glorious minutes lying on your back stretching your hands above your head and pointing your toes in the opposite direction without having to go to too much bother. Get into the habit of letting your body feel meltingly soft. Let yourself feel like you are filled with warm gooey gel. It's a delicious way to be!

31. **Glory in all the beauty around you**. Wherever you are, take in what you see. Notice the details and pick out what delights you to focus on. It's all too easy to see what must be done, imperfections, and things that could be better – but there will *always* be those things. When you choose to bring your attention to what provides pleasure and a feeling of wellbeing, you will be a nicer person to be around, and happier within yourself. Train yourself to have this be a habit. Practice being your own ray of sunshine and see how much better life can get.

32. **Set up a hot beverage station**. Whatever your preferred cozy drink is, set up a petite tray with your favourite cups, pretty teas or delicious coffees. I've always admired this detail in others homes, so I created one for myself. It brings me such pleasure to serve myself tea from this in the morning, and coffee

in the afternoon. And the added bonus is that if you have guests staying, they can feel free to help themselves to a drink as well. It's such a simple idea which doesn't really cost anything since you're bound to have everything you need already. I use a wooden box that a gift set came in and it fits my small selection of teas and coffees perfectly.

33. **Create *hygge* with candles**. *Hygge* is the Danish word for a feeling of coziness and snuggling up. Candles were lit and put in the windows for school children coming home after school since it was already dark during their long, cold winters. Candles are charming in the winter, I agree, but have you considered lighting candles in the summer too? There is something so soothing about the flickering flame. I like tea light candles in pretty candle glasses for their ease of use and no mess. And a scented candle is lovely to have on as well. There are all price points when it comes to candles and for less than $1 you can have a tea light flickering away on the coffee table. Candles really add something to a room!

34. **Indulge in year-round *hygge***. It's easy to cozy up in the winter with a fire in the grate, soft throw rugs on the sofa, and the rain pattering outside. And to dress with a big, soft scarf, wrap up in a warm coat and feel that

27

sense of coziness when it's freezing. But the warmer months are also ripe for a sense of comfort and pleasure. My favourite ways to be *hygge* in the summer are: a light-weight throw rug for the evening when I'm sitting outside, candles as in my previous tip, choosing clothing and loungewear that is soft against my skin, wearing colours that make me feel happy (currently soft-bright shades), and playing my favourite soft background music at home or an engrossing audiobook in the car. What could you add into your day for a feeling of *hygge* no matter the season?

35. **Look up *yin yoga* on YouTube**. I've always known that I 'should' stretch my body more, but it wasn't until I came across yin yoga that I saw how it could be such a rejuvenating practice, and feel wonderfully stretched and relaxed afterwards. I found out about it when I had a yoga studio membership and was trying different classes, but after that expired I looked up yin yoga on YouTube and found classes there. Yin yoga is simply a series of yoga poses done as long stretches, with each stretch lasting anywhere from two to seven minutes. After one of these classes you will feel nicely zen, and your body will feel unbelievably relaxed. I've even done it for myself by simply holding stretches for two minutes each, with the timer on my phone set so I can relax into

the stretch without checking for the time. And of course, setting the timer sound to play relaxing tinkling bells when it is time to go to my next stretch. It's so enjoyable and even fifteen minutes will give you a wonderful feeling afterwards.

36. **Simplify your décor for ease of living**. Even though I love having my favourite possessions around me, I don't like feeling overwhelmed by 'too much stuff' or the suffocating feeling of clutter. One day I imagine I'll have a highly simplified home with pale-coloured walls and a feeling of airy lightness. I can just sense this is how my next home will look. But in the meantime I am enjoying my layered 'Ralph Lauren on a budget' style, at the same time as simplifying a little. I'm not buying any new items. I am enjoying using up consumables. I am passing on objects that no longer ring my bell. And I am having less on display as well. If you too love your décor style but want a relaxed and harmonious feeling, try donating items that no longer feel like 'you', reading books and giving them away, and having a smaller, curated range of décor articles on display. You really can have the best of both worlds this way.

37. **Keep up little home details that delight you**. Some ladies buy themselves an

inexpensive bouquet of flowers each week. I go through phases of this depending on what is available and how much they cost. But something I never fail to do in my environment is to change my hand towels daily, and my pillow slips twice a week (once when I change the sheets, and once in between changes). Doing this creates only a miniscule amount of extra laundry but these two details bring me so much happiness I can't say! It's a pleasure to always dry my hands on a clean towel, and I love having fresh pillow slips more often too. Find areas like this in your home (or borrow mine) and create a little extra luxury for yourself.

38. **Decide that everything gets to be easy** (even the big things). Whatever you've made 'hard' for yourself, *let it now be easy.* Paying off debt, losing weight, simplifying your closet and your home, reading more, writing your first book, even moving house. Just decide that you are willing to accept ease and flow in your life and live from that place. I know for myself it's only because I've decided in my mind that certain things are going to be difficult that they are. Social situations, self-improvement changes we want to make, everything can be much, much easier – and enjoyable even – when we let them be.

39. **Give up the habit of comparing yourself with others**. The more you put your blinkers on (like horses wear!) the happier you will be. Of course you will be kind to others and enjoy social interactions, but put the focus more on what *you* are doing. See how you can enrich your own life rather than seeing what everyone else is doing and maybe feeling less than because of this. I like to be inspired, but sometimes I can find myself being pulled towards activities or items that aren't really 'me'. Try new things for sure, but always look within for your own threads of happiness. My husband Paul always says to 'follow the breadcrumbs' and it's so true. Take note of what lights you up and do more of those things, and you will find the habit of unhelpful comparison will simply fall away. In addition, people will be drawn to *you*, because you always seem to be bright and cheerful, with something new to say!

40. **Keep your goals within a one-day timeframe**. Think about upgrades you've wanted to make in the past such as getting fitter or starting a side hustle. Have any of these things been on your goals list for *years* like they have for me? You wanted to write your first book by the end of the year, or lose weight before a vacation four months away. Instead of placing an arbitrary date on

anything you'd like to achieve, just look at *today*. Plan to do something today that will lead you towards your desired outcome. Write for thirty minutes. Put together a healthy and delicious evening meal and have a coffee afterwards instead of dessert. Do a Pilates class on YouTube after work. Whatever you plan, show up for it. And then, make another plan for tomorrow. Don't stress yourself with deadlines, simply do what you said you would do each day and you will be stepping into your new reality, one day at a time. *If you keep on going, you will get there.*

41. **Schedule maintenance**. Whether it's your body, your home or your car, put everything you can think of onto your calendar. I like to tint my eyebrows every 3-4 weeks, but often longer can go by and I haven't done them. I only notice when I go to put my makeup on and have to spend extra time on my brows. So, I put a recurring memo in my iPhone calendar to tint my brows every three weeks. When it comes up, I do them. It's only a ten-minute job but I simply forget. It's the same with household tasks. We get cobwebs on the outside of our house, especially in the summer, and they really bother me. So I've put a weekly reminder on my calendar to walk around the house with a brush and sweep them down. Again, it's only a ten-minute job, but I forget to

do it and only notice when I'm running out the door or already busy doing another task such as hanging out the laundry. It will make your life feel so much calmer when all these little tasks are under control, so take note of small things that bother you and put them into your schedule. It's also very satisfying deleting the reminders once that task is done!

42. **Research new ideas**. Look up slow living, minimalism, voluntary simplicity or living a soft life. These are all different angles in which to simplify and slow down, and you will find that one or two may resonate more than others. I love the thought of minimalism but sometimes people go further than I am willing to, so I temper it with thoughts of living a soft life and creating order in my home. Helena Woods talks about slow living on YouTube, and she even has a French angle which is lovely. Where you start isn't necessarily where you will finish either. You might begin by learning about minimalism then find something different through *that* search. By starting out at all, you are led to similar ideas which might suit your sensibility better. Follow concepts that pique your interest and be excited and curious about where they might lead you.

43. **Think 'cozy vibes' no matter the season**. What kinds of details make you feel comforted, safe, and happy? Identify yours, and make sure to include them in your daily life, even if you feel they are a bit silly. It's 'your life, your way' and you get to live it how you want. When I'm watching a movie and I notice something they are doing that appeals, I make a mental note. It's always the simple pleasures I find – going for a meander through town and browsing a bookshop, fluffing up my living room before I settle in for a warm-feeling series such as *Sweet Magnolias* on Netflix, or taking my dogs for a walk at a beautiful local dog park and seeing the leaves turning for the autumn season. Start a 'cozy vibes' list for yourself and see how happy it makes you feel.

44. **Listen to your feelings**. Just as you are picking up on good feelings while gathering 'cozy vibes' in the previous tip, so too listen out for not-so-good feelings. When I feel overwhelmed or anxious, it's often because my environment needs straightening up. It means the 'inventory' levels of my home has gotten too high (thanks to Dawn from *The Minimal Mom* on YouTube for the inventory idea!) I have a good tidy up and clean out by donating a few items. I always feel so much better when I get my inventory levels under control. When you experience uncomfortable feelings, tune in

with yourself and ask, 'What is making me feel like this right now?' What situation or event? And how can you make it even a little bit better or preferably, face it head on?

45. **Look within for what lights you up**. In addition to researching interesting ideas, follow your own desires and create your ideal way to live from there. *Look within for the answers*. Journal and ask yourself how your ideal life would look, what is your preferred 'speed', and what kinds of things can you imagine yourself doing if you allowed yourself to live a softer, calmer life where your peace of mind was top priority? List bullet points of everything you come up with and see how even just picturing it in your mind has a soothing effect on you.

46. **Surround yourself with beautiful things**. No matter the aesthetic you are most drawn to – and maybe it is a mix unique to you – let yourself be enfolded in all that you find delightful. Mix in colours you admire in magazines, whether it is for your bedding or your wardrobe. Have a home that is clean and bright and peaceful. Don't worry about trends; let your heart choose for you. Listen to the inner you when she points something out. Tidy up often and arrange everyday items in a pleasing manner. Look on Pinterest or browse

big glossy picture books for ideas, and emulate them using what you have. You don't need an actual Chanel bag and designer jeans to recreate an outfit look, shop your closet and make your own version. Enjoy being creative!

47. **Choose gentle media**. When I am intentional about softening the hard edges of life, I lose myself in a chick lit book, Danielle Steel novel, or Hallmark-style movie. I don't care if they are light and fluffy (although someone often dies unexpectedly in a Danielle Steel book I have found!) If they make me happy, they make me happy. Sometimes you're just not in the mood for a realistic, gritty, crime novel you know? (But I do love a good psychological thriller occasionally.) What I do know is that what I take into my mind affects me, and if I take in quieter, kinder media, it helps me feel safe, secure, and relaxed. The world is scary enough without us adding to it.

48. **Let yourself go jelly-like**. At night when you are falling asleep, or even during the day if you are feeling tense, take a few minutes to close your eyes and breathe a few deep breaths. As you breathe in and out, feel your shoulders relax. Take a few more breaths and imagine your whole body is filled with gel. Feel it flow into your arms and legs, and your torso.

Let your fingertips and toes tingle as the gel circulates. Mine doesn't have a specific colour, just a feeling, but you might like to imagine a lovely colour, or sparkly glitter even. It only takes a few minutes to do this, and you can do it in bed at night, on public transport, at work or wherever. It's such a lovely practice, so remember to be soft and gooey often!

49. **Choose softness as your new standard**. Living a softer life is not just about having everything perfect and thinking there will never be a problem. This unrealistic thought might stop you from thinking it is possible for you to relax into living the way you desire. In life, we will always have issues, both big and small, but when you take on being calm, measured, and down-to-earth as your default, you will be able to handle problems more easily. Don't fall into victim mode and wonder 'why do these things always happen to me?' because problems happen every day to everyone. It's part of being human. Just know that your only job is to choose to live in a softer way, and that it is fully possible for you to do so.

50. **Splurge a little sometimes**. I have always loved taking good care of my skin twice a day and applying a little makeup each morning. I prided myself on not using expensive items,

but at the same time coveted the Estée Lauder brand, right from when I was a teen in the nineteen-eighties. I bought items here and there when there was a Gift with Purchase, but never fully used their products. Then, one day about a year ago I decided, *You know what? I'm in my fifties now and no longer have to watch every penny like I did when I was younger. What am I waiting for, my old age?* On that day I decided I was going to be an 'Estée Lauder girl'. As things have run out I've replaced them with an Estée Lauder product. It still feels like I am doing something naughty, but I'm getting used to it. Others might use this brand without a second thought, but for someone who has always considered herself thrifty, financially savvy, and 'good with money', it's been a bit of a stretch mentally. But I'm happy to be enjoying a luxurious experience twice a day, and also, it doesn't have to be forever. I get to change my mind at any time. Is there something you've considered to be 'out of your league' that you can indulge in perhaps?

51. **Do one thing at a time**. Yes I know, this is a common piece of advice, but wow, when you take heed? Magic happens. Time opens up for you! You get just as much done and maybe even more. And as you work through your day you will feel calm, relaxed, and secure.

Everything that needs to be finished will be. Being fully present and engrossed in the task to hand is the biggest gift you can give yourself. When your mind is no longer juggling multiple jobs there is less chance of making mistakes or missing things. I have to remind myself often, 'Finish this Fiona, complete it and then we can go onto the next thing.' You won't find mysterious half-done tasks around the place, and your environment will be so much more relaxing to be in!

52. **Live like a Hallmark movie character**. I love these cheery, cheesy movies throughout the year and especially at Christmas. The main character has a cutesy creative job, wears red a lot, and is enthusiastic and naïve about life. She doesn't seem weighed down by serious problems (and if there are any they are resolved within ninety minutes). It really is fun to float through their world of an evening! But how can we translate this seemingly perfect Hallmark way of life to our own, more real, earthly experience? What are the takeaways we can apply to our own life? How about dressing the part in clothes that bring us joy with their comfort and pretty colours, as detailed earlier in this book (tip number six). Or being kinder and more cheerful to ourselves and others. We could spend time doing things we enjoy such as handcrafts,

baking, reading, or sipping a hot coffee. We would deal with any issues, and try not to let them weigh on us. Sometimes we can focus too much on what's difficult or dreary in life rather than the good things, when we all have the choice of which direction to look in. When you are having a blah time, infusing your day with the essence of a Hallmark character might be just the tonic.

53. **Run your errands in a softer way**. We all have errands to run, and some of them won't be fun, but there are ways we can enjoy ourselves as well as tick everything off our list. Firstly, give yourself time to do everything so you won't feel rushed, if possible. And if you are short on time, don't panic your brain. Simply tell yourself you have plenty of time, and you'll get everything done. Secondly, make your journey pleasant. Play an audiobook in the car, or listen to one with headphones if you are walking or on public transport. Take water with you to sip on. And if you have to wait in line? Decide you are going to feel calm and relaxed, and zone out into your own little world. Perhaps you are thinking about the style vibe of your next season's wardrobe... Once you have completed your errands, is there a small reward you can buy yourself? A bar of high-quality chocolate? A seasonal beverage? A book or magazine, or even a new

nail polish or handcream? Or maybe there is a specific item you need to replace in your closet and you could use that purchase as your treat.

54. **Do little things you enjoy, even if they cost money**. I have spent so many years being thrifty that it is sometimes difficult to let myself spend 'frivolously', even on small things which would bring me pleasure. I'm talking about ordering coffee at Starbucks (which I might have twice a year and that's with a coupon, when I know others have it many times a week), choosing a paperback book from a bookstore, buying a pretty jigsaw, beautiful gourmet chocolates, fresh flowers, or even a new top. None of these things in themselves cost a lot of money, and if you 'shop' from your list of favourites sparingly you're not going to bankrupt yourself. But there is just something hugely pleasurable about buying something just because you want it; or of giving yourself a small gift every now and again.

55. **Do life your own way**. Even though I have made a few changes in what I spend my money on as outlined in the previous tip, I also like to remain true to myself with my underlying self-described financial savviness. I might buy a Starbucks coffee for the experience once in a while as I said, but most of the time I make my

own at home. I might buy a new book if I see something, but I also use the public library, as well as reading the unread books on my Kindle and bookshelves at home. My purchases are the cherry on top of my enjoyment. You might want to add small items into your budget, but you can also appreciate what you can do for 'free' and take pleasure in that.

56. **Be relaxed and zen**. When you take control over your life and decide to be who you are, you will find yourself more enthused about keeping your everyday details tidy – organizing and cleaning your home, having a not-too-full schedule and doing things ahead of time so that you feel spacious and relaxed. It's almost as if time opens up and you have more of it. On days like this I feel so wonderful it's almost as if I've taken the best full-body (and mind) sedative. And it's all because I've chosen to slow down, feel calm, do jobs one at a time, and enjoy the process instead of rushing to get to the end of the task. It really is the most magical thing!

57. **Have a gentle peacefulness in your demeanour** and how you approach things. Take on a sense of calmness in whatever you are doing at a particular time. Move slower and more deliberately. Let your mind clear and focus on what you are doing. Write down

anything that pops into your mind that you need to remember, or put it in your phone's calendar to do at another time. Just reminding yourself to feel peaceful and calm really does change the way your body operates. You feel your shoulders drop and instinctively take a deep breath. Give yourself the gift of ease and peace at any moment.

58. **Treat your body like a separate person**. If you are someone who has a fraught body image and causes stress to yourself by not eating in moderation, consider your body as a loved friend who is distinct from your head, your mind, and your thoughts. Ask 'her' (your body) what she would like when you get the urge to eat. Too often, I have found that my head overrules my body when I want to eat something. Then I eat 'whatever' and get annoyed with myself (my body) for putting on weight. But it's not my body's fault! She is trying to tell me what she wants, and I haven't always listened in the past. It's always my head (my thoughts on what is a treat, and what I want to taste) that decides, rather than my body. She just follows along, and then gets told off. How unfair! When I *have* sought her input, she has indicated to me that she is feeling good right now and would just like a glass of water. Or, after my breakfast smoothie one day she didn't want a cup of coffee, she wanted to wait

a few hours and have it later in the morning. Or she desired something light, delicious, and hydrating for lunch (such as a salad) rather than perhaps a stodgy, heavy option. It really was quite fascinating and something I am now committed to. When you start doing this it feels wonderful to listen to your body, consider her, respect her, love her, and want the best for her.

59.   **Thank yourself**. To treat yourself as well as you treat others, thank yourself often. And do it aloud. Maybe in a whisper around others, but still. *Thank you for taking me for a walk outside today. Thank you for staying calm when that customer was being unreasonable. Thank you for keeping our closet lovely and tidy. Thank you for doing what you said you were going to do today. Thank you for our lovely early night. Thank you for being you.* Sure it may sound a little silly, but when you appreciate yourself and acknowledge that you've actually done well today, you will feel happier and more content. Sometimes I think that getting through life and enjoying it is a string of little mind tricks. And this is a good one!

60.   **Spend time with a soft pastime**. Hobbies are the perfect way to cultivate softness and a sense of peace in your everyday life. Whether

it's something you have always wanted to try, or a hobby you have enjoyed in the past and for some reason stopped doing, today is the perfect time to begin. In the past I have enjoyed handcrafts such as knitting, patchwork and quilting, sewing, and needlepoint. Recently I started doing jigsaws. I always saw them as a bit pointless in the past, but now I see the appeal. You can choose a pretty picture that you like, and then enjoy the slow, meditative process of putting it together. There is no deadline, and you can do as little or as much at one time. Sundays always seem to be made for jigsaws for me, so I always do at least a little on a Sunday. I bought a large piece of art board from an art supplies store too, so I can move it out to the dining table and then take it away again when it's time for dinner. When I have a jigsaw in progress, I mostly leave it on our hall table; that way I can look for a few pieces when passing. What kind of soft pastime appeals to you?

61. **Ignite your journal time**. Some of my favourite times I've spent recently have been with a book and a journal. It's something that is always shown on Pinterest or Instagram posts, a girl sitting in a café writing in her notebook. But it can be hard to get started sometimes; what to write about, I get it! I've found extra inspiration when I combine my

journal time with a book. I choose something from my shelf that appeals at the time and start out by taking a few notes from the material. Often this then springboards off into my own inspiration. It's so fun to choose a book and settle in for a little thought work, and I'm always thrilled with the results: personalized inspiration, what could be better?

62. **Take your time**. Quit rushing around for good. It's a practice for sure, but just remind yourself every day to slow it down, and give yourself time to complete things. You probably already know that cortisol is damaging to your health, and that you may even burn yourself out if you are constantly in the habit of feeling behind, hurrying, and always trying to catch up. Sometimes it's simply a matter of being intentional about feeling calm and in control, and sometimes it's a practical thing such as giving yourself more time to get somewhere, or complete a task. There is no bigger lifestyle upgrade you can choose than a feeling of space and calm.

63. **Combine errands, tasks, and jobs**. When batching like things together, you will find that even mundane activities feel more enjoyable because you are being efficient with your time. You can actually feel it! I have a running list of

errands that require me to go out in my car, and I put them off until something absolutely needs to be done, or I'm going out to meet someone for a coffee or lunch. It's a better use of petrol *and* my time. Plus, I feel more calm and contented because I'm not always running out for just one errand. Batching is often used in a business sense, but it works wonderfully at home as well. Cooking more than one portion of a meal, or doing all your mending jobs at once are examples of batching. Identify areas in your life that could benefit from this!

64. **Keep your financial life organized**. There is nothing that will help you sleep more at night than knowing where your money is at, and that all your important paperwork is in one file (and you know where that file is!) This is one of those jobs that feels too boring, but for a small amount of time each week you can get – and keep – on top of things. I have a recurring reminder in my phone on a Monday to 'balance bank accounts'. I check through everything, look at payments coming out, and transfer money if needed. When I have a little more time, or more likely am in the mood, I'll do some shredding of old documents and streamline any paperwork. Less comes in the mail these days but there still seems to be a lot of paper. I used to keep everything, but now I only keep the essentials. That way there is less

to sort through to find something. And when you file weekly, you will never find yourself with a daunting mountain of paper.

65. **Create a menu of options**. Imagine having a big list of self-identified simple pleasures to choose from each day. You could have an activities list where you write down everything that makes you feel good, such as going for a walk outside for twenty minutes, having a coffee in a café, washing and blow-drying your hair, getting a manicure or pedicure (at home or out), or reading a book. Note down everything you enjoy and keep this list handy to inspire pockets of rest and recuperation. Try for one-hundred, and title the list (with your own name!) 'Fiona's 100 Simple Pleasures'. What a fun project this would be to build. Imagine settling in for a journal session to find *your* one-hundred, and then the fun of 'shopping' from it!

66. **Be intentionally softer**. I love the phrase 'soft life', where the focus is to create a soft, stress-free experience for yourself, where you choose a lifestyle of comfort and relaxation. How can you build this into your everyday? Are there parts of your day where there is always a crunch that you can change up? In addition, can you designate a day or two each week to be 'soft life' days? Where you have a

day of rest, doing exactly as you please? Even if you have jobs to do, you can still choose to complete them in a softer way, by giving yourself adequate time, not rushing, humming a favourite song to yourself or simply breathing in and out and enjoying feeling calm while you work.

67. **Go into the week fresh**. Spend a day dealing with all those little jobs and loose ends that *prevent* you from living a soft life. Sort of like prepping for your week on a Sunday. For me that would mean reconciling my bank accounts, changing my bed sheets, ensuring all my laundry is up to date, mapping out my coming week's appointments and listing things I'd like to get done in my planner. Plus answering any emails and completing small tasks. The days when I wrap up a ton of little chores I feel so good. Each one was like a tiny weight hanging over me and now they are gone. Think about how much energy would be freed up if you did this regularly.

68. **Keep a lady basket**. I've mentioned this before in my book '30 Chic Days at Home, Vol. 2', but it needs to be discussed here, because nothing promotes living a lovely life quite like a lady basket does. Simply put, a lady basket is a container to house a small number of items that you like to have around you. I used to

carry a teetering stack around the house, and it was my husband Paul who observed one day, 'You need something to carry that all around in' and that was how the lady basket was born. In mine I have my Kindle, iPad and phone. A journal and pen. Lip balm, and handcream in a tube. A nail file. My reading glasses. The novel I'm currently reading. Yours might also contain breath mints, an individually wrapped chocolate, or a small needlework project. Make sure to clean it out regularly, because they can get quite full! I know you will love having a lady basket too, and I'm sure you will be able to find something around the house to use as *your* lady basket.

69. **Look for moments of magic**. Often I find myself listening to an audiobook when the narrator mentions the *exact* thing I am doing at the time, or it's something that has recently happened in my life. I am quite tickled by these coincidences, and since I told Paul about it he finds it happens to him too, but with movies and television shows. Sometimes he will just look at me with an incredulous look on his face when it happens! Other moments of magic are seeing a beautiful sky when I step outside, coming across a black and white feather on the ground (it's my dad's way of stopping in to say 'Hi' from heaven), and having a fantail bird flitting back and forth outside my office

window, flirting with me! But it wasn't until I started appreciating all these little things that I started noticing them more. It's fun to look out for them now. What are your personal moments of magic?

70. **Choose your era**. I love the current trend for calling everything an era. You can be in your calm era, your soft girl era, your peaceful era, your money era, or your me-but-better era. It is said to have been popularised by Taylor Swift with her Eras tour, and it's basically another way to say 'phase'. But more fun! What era are you in now? For me, I'm in my happy girl era, my writing era, my creativity era and my organized era. It's good to have a focus or two, and more enjoyable to give them cute era names. And another thing I love about the era trend is that it's okay to change your mind about things. What you be, do or have now isn't set in stone for the rest of your life. It's just an era you are in. You get to evolve and try new things!

71. **Choose your aesthetic**. The clean girl aesthetic. The vanilla aesthetic. The soft girl aesthetic. The Cottagecore aesthetic. The 90s aesthetic. There are popular aesthetics like these, but you can make up any aesthetic that you like. It's a fun way of naming the style you are going for right now. I love the 90s

aesthetic, *Victoria* magazine aesthetic, Hallmark aesthetic as already mentioned, and I love a good Danielle Steel 90s miniseries aesthetic complete with red nail polish and a classic perfume. Choose a few aesthetics that appeal and shape your clothing, book and music choices around them. Dip into one on a day when you need a little energy boost. Search on Pinterest for extra inspiration on your particular aesthetic, and find new ones too!

72. **Reduce things that stress you**. There are two ways you can make your life feel calmer and less dramatic. The first is to change things around you. This looks like simplifying your home, setting boundaries and upholding them in a kind yet firm way, and opting out of tasks that feel heavy on you. The second is to change the way you react to others. You can choose to be less annoyed by people ('it's just how they are'). You can also decide that you are no longer going to get worked up by the little things. These two decisions will go a long way towards lowering your stress levels and allowing you to live in a more peaceful way. Wishing circumstances were different (that you have no power to change) is the opposite of peaceful.

73. **Rely on yourself**. You can't depend on anyone else to gift you with the soft, calm way of living you desire. Even if they are the kindest and most generous person around. It all has to come from within – from your ideas, your wishes, and your actions. When you see yourself as taking charge and putting little changes into place to enable yourself to live in a different way, you start making progress instead of feeling unhappy 'with your lot'. You stop waiting around for others to do things for you. You feel more positive. You know that it's possible! Don't wait around for permission. Give it to yourself and start shaping your beautiful life today.

74. **Be inspired by others** who have what you want. 'Copy' them in a way that is authentic to you. One lady I used to work with talked about her peaceful evening routine. She was a little older than me, married, and she and her husband had never had children. She spoke of dinner with her husband at the table each night, and how she would spend quiet time before bed washing her face and applying a mask. She even invited me around for dinner one evening and her home was just as lovely as I imagined. She was so elegant and poised, that I subconsciously took on many of the things she spoke about. I still remember her vividly

and I worked with her more than twenty years ago. Thank you dear Christine!

75. **Be a brightly lit person**. Brian Tracy said, 'The more positive, optimistic and cheerful you are, the more people will want to be around you and help you in any way possible.' I have found this too, both when I am drawn to people, and how others are when I am cheery. One lady I see each week at the supermarket always has a big genuine smile, and I always enjoy chatting with her. Getting along well with people always makes me feel good, so I try to remember Brian's advice as much as I can. And, optimism feels wonderful for me too. As well, I find myself in solution mode rather than complaining mode when I am in a cheerful mood.

76. **Be honest and truthful**, even in the small things. Something that has aways helped me feel calm and peaceful is to live in integrity. Trying to 'get away with' something, or being dishonest even in a tiny way, feels horrible. The few times I've thought of something inconsequential, 'Oh it won't matter', I realise *it does*. It does because it eats away inside at you. Your higher self is not happy with you and she is showing it by the way you feel. It's just not worth it. Life is better when you dwell in truth. 'You're never wrong to do the right

thing' is a motto I like to live by. I heard this in 'The Intern' movie spoken by Robert de Niro's character Ben, referencing Mark Twain, and it's a good one!

77. **Find a way of living that makes you truly happy**. One day recently I was having a lovely day. It wasn't anything special, just my everyday happenings, but it flowed well, I was getting things done, and I felt content. I said to my husband later on how nice it and been, and remarked, 'I love a simple life where you do simple things and enjoy them.' Luckily he concurred, because he loves a peaceful and relaxed existence also. Maybe in the past I felt like I should have been more of a go-getter, but now I know myself better. I love to live a simple and straightforward life, seeing the people I love and doing things I enjoy doing. If this sounds good to you, borrow it, and if not, design your own. Think about the times you've been the most thrilled with life, and work out how to make that your everyday, or at least the essence of. If you love travelling, can you make it your permanent life? Can you work remotely? Or can you travel at home as well as when you go away, through books, movies, YouTube tours and documentaries? We really do have limitless abundance when it comes to how we live our everyday lives! Isn't it wonderful?

78. **Have amnesia**. When we first viewed our current home, my husband and I were taken with the view. We couldn't tear our eyes away! It's still beautiful several years later, but we do sometimes take it for granted, I know. So we try to remember how it felt that first time, and make everyday viewings like the first time. And so too is it beneficial to do this with the people you love. Bring new eyes to a relationship. Come in fresh and appreciate all the little things about someone. Forget past bickerings and be new every day. Be new with yourself too. Forget about how you were yesterday and decide who you want to be today. Every day gets to be a clean slate if you want it to. Try it for yourself and see how light you feel in your spirit.

79. **Seek simple, soothing energy**. I used to attract chaotic people like a magnet. Was there something in me that they needed? I do know that I love to help people out and have gotten personally involved when someone seemed in need (sometimes to my detriment unfortunately). But I saw it had spread to people I hired or paid for their services as well. Some resolved themselves by moving away or changing their own circumstances, and some, in service provider situations, I left. I decided this one day after I came home from a hair appointment. During this appointment I sat

there the whole time listening to my hairdresser complain about her life, and when I commented to be polite, she didn't even hear me and kept on talking! And of course I paid her quite a lot at the end for my highlights and trim. Yes, I received the service I'd paid for, but I hadn't had a lovely time relaxing with my Kindle as I had done with other hair appointments. That's when I made the choice to only be around people who had simple, light, uplifting energy. People who I could co-exist happily with. I'm happy to report that since this time, life has felt more peaceful, and when I do have an appointment, I thoroughly enjoy it. If you are a sensitive or empathetic person, you may find the same. Don't feel bad about changing who you do business with, it's your money you're spending after all.

80. **Write out your soft, calm ideal day**. I'm sure you have done the 'Ideal Day' exercise before if you love personal development like I do. It's where you write out, you guessed it, your ideal day, from the time you wake up right through to the end of the day. You describe how you look and feel, who you live with, what you home looks like, what you do for work during the day and how you dine, as well as your demeanour and how you interact with the world. It's such a fun journal prompt, so why not create an intentionally *soft, calm,*

blissful ideal day? Apply these filter words and choose whether it is an ideal work day, weekend or vacation day, a special occasion day such as your birthday, Christmas, or a celebration that you look forward to. You can write it as a little story, or sometimes a bullet point list is fun to brainstorm. Get that lovely dreamy, floaty, relaxing feeling in your body, let yourself go loose and soft, and create a soft, calm ideal day for yourself.

81. **Flirt with life**. Do you sometimes wake up with a feeling of dread or heaviness in the morning, even though you love your life generally? Me too, and it's silly. It's only my doom-filled mind that does this and I don't need to listen to her. And you don't either. Instead, why not choose to flirt with life? To see life as a playground rather than a battleground? We'd still get things done that need to get done, but alongside that why wouldn't we choose to feel light and playful and, yes, maybe even a little flirtatious? It's a choice that we probably don't even think of, we just think how we wake up is how we wake up. I can see for myself that if I chose to flirt with my day, I'd have a little pep in my step, I'd dress differently, and the words I'd speak and the tone of my voice would be different too. Are you willing to try it for a day with me? Of course you are! It will be fun!

82. **Connect with others in a way that suits you**. I am happiest when by myself, and often at home, but that doesn't preclude me from enjoying seeing others. Over the years I've realized that I enjoy certain social experiences more than others. I prefer going out for lunch rather than in the evening, and having people around for dinner at home instead of a restaurant. I also love hosting ladies afternoon tea. A friend and I used to meet to watch a movie at a theatre on a Saturday afternoon and it was such an enjoyable visit. We'd have coffee afterwards and discuss the movie as well as catch up on our lives. Decide for yourself how you most enjoy seeing others, and plan for something soon.

83. **Give up people-pleasing**. I didn't *think* I was a people-pleaser; I thought I had a solid sense of myself. But when I looked into it, I discovered I totally tiptoed around some people so I wouldn't upset them. I'd also bend to their wishes and do whatever they preferred. It caused low-lying resentment in me and must have felt quite smothering to them. So, one day I tried out 'being me'. I was kind and soft, of course, but I started speaking up more for what I preferred, did things without checking in with others, and generally started pleasing myself. It's still a work in progress but the more I do it, the better it feels.

You need to get over the 'Am I selfish?' aspect first, and that can still crop up for me, but it's worth persevering with. I look upon this as being *self-possessed* which is described online as someone who is 'calm and confident and in control of their emotions'. I think that sounds pretty good, don't you?

84. **Cultivate self-love**. Many of us are hard on ourselves. We have impossibly high standards (that we never seem to reach) and nothing we do is ever good enough. Imagine instead loving yourself exactly as you are. I'm willing to bet, that instead of things falling apart, your life will *blossom*. Sure you've made mistakes in the past, but who hasn't? Give yourself the grace to start over. Know that your value lies in more than how you look or what you do. Take opportunities as they are presented or create your own. I heard a lady on YouTube talk about how she felt like working out more and really enjoying exercise when she practiced self-love and fell in love with her own self and her body. She just wanted to look after her body and take care of 'her'. I have also started listening to my body and what she requires, and have had the same experience. Our body has wisdom and if we listen, she will share it with us. Doesn't this sound like a wonderfully caring, peaceful and simple way to live?

85. **Take the time to do what you enjoy**
without guilt. I always enjoy the romanticized
ideal of retirement communities (such as
portrayed in the movie 'In Her Shoes'), and I'm
sure they are wonderful in real life too.
Residents have made the big move and
downsized their possessions, as well as their
responsibilities. They have the freedom to do
what they want, when they want. There is time
to read, piece together a puzzle, go for a walk,
and socialize with friends. I won't be moving to
one of these places for at least 15-20 years, but
any of us can practice this peaceful way of life
anytime we like. Plopping down with a book
'just because'. Buying a pretty jigsaw puzzle
and creating the picture with no timeframe to
worry about. Often I find any busy-ness is all
in my head. I tell myself I don't have the time,
but then I spend time on unimportant tasks
such as scrolling online with nothing to show
for it! Analogue activities are more relaxing for
our brain, so won't you join me in a little
downtime? Doing something soft and
pleasurable? We owe it to our mental health.

86. **Enjoy the outdoors**. I'm more an indoor
kind of girl, in that the kinds of things I enjoy
doing are all... inside. That's why I like to be
intentional about going outside each day. To
sit in the sun for a little while or go for a walk
on a dappled leaf day. There is always

something new to see. Nature changes every day. Vitamin D is good for your skin and your eyes. It activates changes in your body and makes you healthier. I'm not talking about sunbathing for hours, but ten or fifteen minutes here and there. When you go outside, you notice the seasons change. You are more in tune with nature, and with yourself. If you often read inside, why not take your book outside, even if it's not summer. One of the coziest things for me to do is sit under our covered patio when it's softly raining and a mild temperature. It gives me good shivers! Right after I finish this tip I'm going to take my doggies for a walk down the road. Being outside makes everyone happy, both people and pets!

87. **Devise a list of active soft activities**. 'The mind should be still and the body active, but most people are the other way around'. I heard this quote a long time ago and it's always stuck with me. That's why it feels much better to be moving our body rather than sitting still for hours (likely doing something involving a screen). Of course at work we can't help it, but in our private life we absolutely can. Considering this prompted me to come up with a list of active ways to relax, including such pastimes as baking, and making greeting cards and gift tags from the pretty bits and

pieces I have saved up. I also like to re-sort my bookshelf and reacquaint myself with my 'old friends' while also releasing a few titles that no longer resonate. Jigsaw puzzles are a nice way to actively relax too, as previously mentioned. And going for a walk at a park always feels good. If you want to spend less time seated, start creating your own list of active ways to enjoy yourself.

88. **Create stability and security for yourself**. Something that definitely belongs in your soft life is a feeling of safeness. A home life you feel protected in, money things sorted, and good people around you. You don't need to be a millionaire, but it will help you relax to know that your bills are paid and you have at least a small emergency account. When I was younger and renting a big house with three other girls, I very quickly realised that spending money mindlessly did not make me feel good. It felt better to put that same money into a savings account so that I never went short or felt stressed. Do this for yourself. Pay yourself first by saving or investing small amounts that you might have otherwise frittered on 'great deals'. Instead of feeling deprived, think to yourself 'I'm paying this money to *me* instead'. It will turn things around in an instant.

89. **Choose 'built for comfort'**. No matter what you are purchasing, make sure it is the softest, most comfortable, easiest-to-use option. Whether you are in the market for a new car, clothes, shoes, or furniture, prioritize *comfort*. Of course you will have to like the look of something as well, but if you put comfort as number one and good looks a close second, you can't go wrong. Think back to items you bought and never used. For me I'm thinking of a couple of pairs of high heels which were just that touch too high, but I thought I'd get used to them. Can you guess that they are in my closet barely used? And the heels that are lower are my most used pairs? We can't force ourselves into wanting to wear something. Well, we can, but the end result is that we're miserable all day. Add ease and happiness into your life by *always choosing to be comfortable*.

90. **Calm your mind**. I have the kind of mind that sometimes feels like a big tangle inside. It is prone to overthinking, and the things that I think will make me feel better often make it worse (such as lying around scrolling on my phone, eating something tasty but trashy – who knew!) Basically, I need to do the opposite of what I feel like – getting active and doing something physical, shutting down my computer, and completing small tasks. Maybe

I'll eat something protein with something fresh, such as a handful of raw nuts and an apple, unsweetened Greek yoghurt, or cheese and crackers. Or for brunch or lunch, scrambled eggs. I also find it helpful to breathe in and out while harnessing my thoughts. Whatever unhelpful commentary is running around, I reframe it to create a positive thought. Sometimes I'll just think to myself 'calm and simple' while I breathe, and that helps too. Whenever you find yourself with a busy mind, stop, redirect it, and then carry on with your day. It makes a huge difference.

91. **Make a skincare routine easy**. Setting up your skincare products to ensure you use them will make a huge difference to your complexion. I have found that I forget about things if I don't have them front and centre – out of sight, out of mind for sure. One example for me is that I bought a primer because I heard others rave about using a primer under your makeup. But I never remembered to use it! So I shifted it from my makeup area to my skincare area. Now, it's right there to put on as a second layer after my day cream each morning. If you want to be more consistent with your skincare, make it easy and set yourself up for success – no stress required.

92. **Create a grooming routine**. If, by the same note, you often forget to pamper yourself with the grooming habits you'd love to do, create a little schedule for yourself. When things become automatic, life feels easier, softer. To start with I wrote them in my planner, but now they have become habitual for me. The difference is I don't let everything slide and then wonder why I feel such a mess. Every month or so I tint my eyebrows, every few weeks I shave my legs (it's winter right now, in the summer I'll do them more frequently), and I use exfoliator on my face in the shower once a week. Whatever you desire to include in your grooming routine, write a little schedule and make sure you do them. Nothing ever takes long, it's the remembering to that can be the issue sometimes!

93. **Let your life be guided** by the principles of authenticity and simplicity, of gentleness and kindness. Each day ensure the wellbeing of your soul by prioritizing your relationship with yourself. What does this mean in a practical sense? Give yourself what you need. Don't push away rest, play or self-care. Some of us can *totally* be the martyr, I know I've done it before. But it serves no-one, least of all you. And it only makes those around us feel bad. You don't need to be selfish; you can simply state what you require from time to time. I

know that even when you're by yourself it can be difficult: 'I don't have time', or 'I have to get this finished'. But you do have time. *Give yourself what you need*. It will all work out.

94. **'Big dreams start with small steps'**. Take small steps towards *your* ideal life, a softer, calmer life where your every wish is granted. Ask yourself, *What are three small things I could do right now towards making my life more enjoyable, and more pleasurable?* What comes to mind for me is relaxing into my body instead of being 'in my head' all the time. And doing things that pop into my thoughts that might be fun instead of ignoring them. Plus, taking on the energy of softness as a default. It doesn't mean I'm going to be a pushover; I live my life in the manner I desire, but I do so in a softer, gentler way. These are all energetic for me, but you may find you receive practical tips from your inner wisdom.

95. **Shop your home**. Similar to shopping your closet, look around your home to find books to read, crafts to work away at, clothes to wear, and makeup to use. I had a lovely few hours yesterday afternoon reorganizing my style files and was inspired as well as tidying up my home office shelves. Most of us will have beautiful items at home that we've become used to. When you take the time to bring them

out, polish them up, and use them in a different setting or even at all, you will have a new appreciation not only for the item, but your abundance as well. Everything will seem fresh, and you won't feel the urge to go and buy something new, thus reducing clutter as well as unnecessary expenditure.

96. **Create your own inspiration** by reflecting in your journal. Look at your current lifestyle and any stress points, and identify places in which you could use a little more softness and calmness. Is there one area you can brainstorm ways in which to be happier and more successful? Simply take your category and write it down, then write underneath, 'How can I have a calmer, softer experience in this area?' Or 'How can I feel more relaxed and happier in this area, what would it take? What are some ideas to try?'

97. **Go for the kind of lifestyle you want**. Identify others who have done it to know that it is possible firstly. Look to them rather than others. Borrow their faith that it's okay to slow down, live simply, and choose a quiet life. Don't let others convince you with their words or their actions, that their (busy, chaotic, stressful) life is the only way to be. They may enjoy it, or perhaps may not know there is another option. Whatever the reason, they get

to live their way. And you get to do you. Keep coming back to your true desires, don't let them be forgotten about. You might choose different words than soft and calm; whatever describes your happy place, keep them front and centre. Base life decisions around them. It's *your* life.

98. **Get out and do all the things** you can imagine yourself doing when you are living your idealistic life. Foreign movies on the big screen, live nights at a local jazz club, visiting museums and galleries, walking through beautiful public gardens, going to the theatre or a comedy show. I'm a total homebody to the point that I can realize sometimes it's been ages since I went to something out of the ordinary, and that's the perfect time to plan something new. Like a vacation, it shakes things up and gives you a fresh perspective.

99. **Inspire those around you** rather than badger them. Don't become so over-enthused about your fun plans that people are turned off. Instead, work your magic through your actions. And actually, you are enjoying yourself so much that you don't need the buy-in of other people. You are receiving a ton of pleasure already. Sure it's enjoyable to share, but more so from a place of people noticing and being drawn to you, rather than by you

chasing them down! Be that magnetic and elusive lady who inspires others by the way she lives. Of course, first you need to work out what that looks like for you, which arguably could be the best part!

100. **Please yourself**. Ultimately, designing your dreamiest life is down to you. No-one else knows you well enough to create it for you. Even while living in imperfect circumstances, you can still craft a wonderful way to live. Take little details and infuse your days with them. Surround yourself with movies and books that delight and uplift you. Colours that make you happy. Food that makes you feel amazing. Answer truthfully when you are asked a preference. This may sound basic, but as someone who has often deferred to others wishes, it feels really strange at first. The good news is that doing so make you happier, helps others respect you more, and is excellent for your self-esteem.

The energy of this book is calm, simple, and maybe even a little slow-paced for some. I know if my brother was reading it he would have fallen asleep in the first few pages! But some of us need plentiful reminders to slow down and relax. We can find it hard to switch off.

If this sounds like you, I invite you to shift into a

different gear. To take an energetic sedative and approach your everyday life this way. There is no need to feel 'behind' all the time, but I know from my own experience it can very much be a habit.

What helped for me was to 'let it all go'. Let everything weighing on my shoulders fall away, trusting that I would know the important things. All any of us can do is our best and that should be good enough.

To thank you for picking up this little book, I wrote fifty extra tips, on the fun topic of romanticizing your everyday, which I think complements living a soft, calm life perfectly.

I hope you enjoy this bonus chapter!

50 Ways to Romanticize Your Everyday

An online description of romanticizing your life said it was to 'think about or describe something as being better or more attractive or interesting than it really is'. And a big part of living a softer, calmer life is making the very best of our everyday. Even with a job, our family and home to look after, plus tasks such as groceries and laundry, we can still make these things enjoyable instead of a never-ending slog.

Right from when I was a little girl I was someone who romanticized the way I lived. I just didn't have a name for it then. People thought I was airy-fairy, flossy, and lived in a dreamworld. But guess what, I didn't even care. I was happy, and from what I saw most people were bored by their life and didn't find it as fun as I did. Each to their own, I thought, and simply carried on with how I did things. After all, we are free to spend our time as we wish, and we are also free to live our life as we please. As long as we are not hurting anyone else, of course!

To encourage you around to my way of doing things, may I present you with fifty little ways you can enhance a feeling of playfulness in your everyday, create and enjoy a more idealistic way of living, and generally look at things through rose-tinted glasses.

Because why not? What could be more fun?

Let's dive in and start to romanticize today, and every day!

1. **Make over your tasks**. Write down your daily activities and have a little brainstorming session about how you can make them more intentional and pleasurable. I used to really resent making my bed and in my mind it took me *ages* to do. But now I know (because I timed myself) that it takes less than five minutes, even when I do it properly. Often I'll be listening to an audiobook too, which feels like a treat while I smooth the sheets and plump the pillows.

2. **Recreate an idea from a magazine or Pinterest**. Whether it's an artfully plated breakfast, laying out on a blanket under a tree to

read in the shade, or arranging your closet so that it resembles a stylish boutique, there are always new inspirations to elevate any area of your life. Next time you come across something that appeals, give it a go straight away.

3. **Learn how to make your favourite drink**. I love an iced coffee when I'm out, but I'd never gathered together the ingredients to make one at home – until now. I researched how to make cold-brew coffee and combine it with milk and ice in a tall glass. Plus whipped cream of course! There are Starbucks recipes on their website, and tons of other recipes as well. Just search for your favourite drink and see what you find.

4. **Curate your mood**. However you desire to be, ensure your surroundings reflect this. My ideal way of living is wholesome, gentle, peaceful, and creative. I listen to cozy and romantic genre audiobooks, play gentle background music, dress in colours that make me feel happy, and endeavour to generate a sense of peace and order in my home.

5. **Create a beautiful environment for yourself**. It doesn't even take much more effort! Often all that's needed is a little inspiration to beautify your surroundings. Tidy up, clean out the trash, corral like items onto pretty trays, and curate an environment that

you love. Do it as if you're expecting guests while you design pretty spaces for yourself.

6. **Eat outside whenever possible**. You might have a tiny table on your balcony or a patio area off the dining room. I like to keep our outdoor area clean and welcoming, and a red geranium in a pot just adds to the ambience. There is something about dining in the fresh air or sipping a drink that enhances the enjoyment of the moment.

7. **Take a daily inventory**. Write down all the tasks you habitually do, and then have a brainstorming session to find out ways in which to make them more enjoyable – romanticize your chores! I hang washing out on the line with an audiobook playing on the phone in my jeans pocket. I listen to an inspiring podcast in the car. I light a scented candle while I write. And I make lemon green tea in my cheery orange Starbucks mug bought in Hawaii and dream of our vacation there while it's pouring with rain outside. My husband Paul likes to play Frank Sinatra while he is putting together a meal or cleaning the kitchen. Whatever you are doing, look for a way in which to increase your pleasure factor.

8. **Make a day of it**. If you have an outing, make the most of it. Today I have a pedicure booked

and I'm really looking forward to relaxing while it is being done. But I'm also planning to go a little earlier and meet my mum for a coffee, browse around the new autumn season fashions, plus check out a few thrift stores too (I love the second-hand book sections). Plus, pick up a few groceries on the way home at a supermarket I don't often get to.

9. **Dress the part**. Make like the heroine of your romantic story and dress like her. Blow-dry your hair, taking the extra ten minutes to take it from 'everyday' to 'bombshell'. Wear a favourite outfit. Spritz on a romantically nostalgic perfume (I have small bottles of Estée Lauder old school originals such as *White Linen* and *Beautiful* precisely for this reason). Present yourself to the world in a way that makes you happy.

10. **Create your mood with music**. Curate the soundtrack to your romantic life. One song that always makes me feel instantly cooler and more insouciant is Nina Simone singing 'Black Coffee'. It's the words, the music, and Nina herself. And the thought of being the kind of lady who drinks black coffee too, even though I have mine with milk to save my teeth from staining!

11. **Make meals more special**. Set the table with a candle and play music in the background. Use cloth or paper dinner napkins and placemats or a tablecloth. Give the television a rest once or twice a week and dine as a family at the table – even if your 'family' is just yourself, or you and your husband as it is for me.

12. **Put your gratitude glasses on**. When you look at your life through the lens of gratefulness and wonder, you greatly enhance your enjoyment of everyday, ordinary life. *Look where I live! See how many lovely books are on my shelves just waiting for me to pick them up! Gosh, how comfortable is my bed, it's fabulous!* Look at your home as if you've just been given it for free and appreciate all the goodness you have. A positive and happy mindset can only lead to greater things.

13. **Every day is a fresh start**. Was yesterday not so good? Did you act like a brat? Say things you regret, either to yourself or others? Well today is a new day. Give yourself the gift of starting over. Become a best friend to yourself and treat yourself with care and attention. Treat yourself to lovely meals, relaxing time, and pampering too.

14. **Become nonjudgmental about your thoughts**, emotions, and physical

circumstances. Notice them, but do not react. Rather, be interested and curious. Perhaps it is 'I feel angry right now': What does this mean? Why? Can you let yourself settle down instead of jumping to an extreme response? Can you simply let yourself feel angry for a little while instead of resisting it? I have found that when I simply let my emotions flow, they move through me quicker.

15. **Don't wait for life to be perfect**, and instead enjoy how things are right now. Likely things will *never* be picture-perfect. Decide to be *perfectly imperfect*. You don't need to impress people by always being proper, correct, and right. Or perfectly coiffed. Of course we always want to show our best side, but on occasions when you do have a human moment, laugh and let it go. Think of it as an endearing chink in your armour. It's okay to be real!

16. **Plan a little picnic**. Whether it's a carpet picnic inside, taking a rug outdoors to your lawn, or going to a public park or beach, there's something so romantic about sitting cross-legged with a few delicious snacky foods and a delicious drink.

17. **Make your meals *vibrant***. Chop a tomato or persimmon – whatever you have in the fruit bowl – and add a different colour to your plate.

My aunt is great at this, and always says that we eat with our eyes. Bright green fresh parsley is another one I love to add too.

18. **Read from paper wherever possible**. We all spend so much time with screens, so choose to read a real book or magazine, or even buy a newspaper every once in a while – the weekend issues have interesting supplements. You will find you take in the information in a different way, and your mind isn't jumping around to the next app, because you only have one option in front of you.

19. **Theme your days**. Choose two or three words to flavour your day. If you're at work, you might choose 'composed and productive'. Or at home, 'feminine, relaxed and sensual'. It's fun to create a master list of appealing descriptive words for yourself to shop from too!

20. **Create a cozy environment**. Identify what brings you comfort and joy, and surround yourself with these things: a soft blanket (thick and warm, or a very fine cotton summer blanket), scented or tealight candles, an essential oil diffuser, and fresh flowers. Make your living space into a cozy sanctuary where you can unwind and relax.

21. **Have a mini makeover**. Refresh yourself by choosing something small to make over. Perhaps you will try a nail polish colour that you never thought you'd wear, or decide to go a little shorter with your long hair instead of 'just a trim'. Maybe you'll like the results, or maybe you will decide, 'actually I was right, I don't like dark blue nails'. But just the act of trying something different will feel invigorating.

22. **Start your day in peace**. After you switch off your alarm but before you get out of bed, lie there feeling the sheets on your body. Take some deep breaths and feel all your limbs relax. Stretch them out where they are and then sink into your bed again. Just a few minutes like this is a really nice start to the day!

23. **Go to a movie**. There is no better way to feel in a fresh mindspace than seeing a movie on the big screen. Whether I go with someone else, or alone (sometimes I can't get anyone else excited about seeing a French-subtitled movie with me!) I always emerge from the theatre feeling like I've been away on a trip, and it's only been a few hours.

24. **Dress for the activity**. I like to put my gym clothes on first thing in the morning, to exercise and then shower. After my shower I put on presentable, comfortable day clothes to wear

while writing at home. Pre-dinner, I love to change into loungewear – glamorous satin pyjamas, and then at bed-time I put on my sleepwear – usually a satin cami set or slip. I love that each change helps me feel a different way – active in the morning, productive during the day, and relaxed in the evening. Are there any tweaks you could make to how you dress at different times of the day?

25. **Keep a list of your current favourite affirmations** on an index card in the drawer by your bed, or even in your lady basket. If you're worried someone will read them, dedicate a tiny notebook to affirmations instead. You may find they 'wear off' or can lose their effectiveness, that's why it's good to use new ones regularly. If you desire to feel 'calm and focused' today, write that down to remember your wish.

26. **Notice the beauty around you**. This is what romanticizing your life is, at it's simplest. So what can you see right now? Do you have a view outside? Even if it's just buildings, you can notice the sky, a far-away tree perhaps, or even birds flying past. If you are at work and can't see a lot to admire, perhaps your handcream tube is beautiful. Train your mind to search for beauty and you will find it.

27. **Make your goals more attractive**. Brainstorm how you can make your current goals more fun, exciting, easier, and more stylish. Let yourself be fanciful as you dream up ideas in your journal!

28. **Take a paper book out with you**. I love Pinterest images where a lady is reading her book at a café, in the park or at the beach. It's just not quite the same with a phone or Kindle, if only for the aesthetics! Keep a book with you so that you too can sit for a moment and read a few pages. Why not recreate that Pinterest vibe for yourself?

29. **Journal away from home**. Along the same lines, take a small journal with you, and perhaps write in that instead. Observe what you see, how you feel, and any chic sightings you may come across. Even just recording your outing could be a gentle way to spend ten minutes.

30. **Be pro-active**. Don't just sit around waiting for your life to become easier, more elegant, and sparklier. Whenever you get an idea, a brain-wave, or hear something that appeals, try it straight away or write it down in your *Ideas* notebook to try soon. Be someone who actively makes their life better.

31. **Change up your energy**. When you shift your energy, *everything* shifts. Putting yourself in a more effervescent state of mind can be instantaneous, and it lifts all areas of your life. Imagine fizzy bubbles rising inside you, maybe it's champagne, maybe it's a babbling brook. Feel excited for today and every day. Let yourself feel light and happy!

32. **Romanticize health**. Joseph Pilates said 'Physical fitness is the first requisite of happiness'. If you would like to improve your health, look at ways it can be more pleasurable. I have learned to enjoy exercise by walking outdoors with an audiobook, and finding a Pilates channel I like on YouTube (Move With Nicole). These two things make me feel like I'm on a rich lady spa retreat!

33. **Do it for yourself**. It doesn't matter if others might not be interested in romanticizing the mundane, *you are*. When I think too much about what others might think of a plan, it affects my enthusiasm. Don't let this happen to you. Just act on a whim and choose to sing an aria while you do your chores, pretending that you live in Sicily. It doesn't even matter if you don't know a song and can't speak Italian. Make up your own or change your favourite pop song into an operatic masterpiece!

34. **Transport yourself somewhere else** for the day, or the weekend. Choose a theme such as 'Paris in the Winter', and dress as if, listen to French music you enjoy, and lose yourself in a novel set in Paris. I just finished listening to 'The Paris Connection' (called 'Uncoupling' in the US) by Lorraine Brown and it was such a lovely read. A different mental backdrop will have you feeling refreshed, inspired, and loving your life again.

35. **Be intentional with your lighting**. Turn on lamps during the day, light candles or use flameless LED candles, and make the most of natural light. There is a place for overhead lighting, but use it sparingly, and definitely lower the lights after dinner to relax your mind before bedtime.

36. **Enjoy 'hostess' touches**. Buy yourself an inexpensive packet of cocktail napkins in your favourite colour and use these to serve guests – or yourself – a drink on, hot or cold. Mine are black and cost $2.50 for a packet of fifty from the dollar store. I love the five-star hotel touch they add!

37. **Romanticize the season**. As I write this, it's the first few days of winter, so last night I spent a lovely half hour brainstorming all the ways I could have a beautiful winter and the types of

things I would enjoy doing. I felt very calm and relaxed before bed from doing this, and I also now have a delightful winter wishlist.

38. **Change something you don't like doing** into something you might actually look forward to, all by the power of your mind. If you have to see a relative who always niggles at you, take this as an opportunity to act as a benevolent duchess in town for the day. Take the high road!

39. **Create ambience wherever you go**. At work, at home, and in your car too are all places in which you probably spend plenty of time, so make them nice places to be with the finishing touches that bring you happiness. You can also create 'ambience' within yourself: with posture, good energy, and a smile.

40. **Enjoy being a feminine and polished lady**. Keeping this phrase in mind makes me feel cheerier, increases my productivity in a gentle way, and helps me feel at peace. Borrow it for yourself if you like: *I enjoy being a feminine and polished lady*. Or reword it to suit your sensibility if it doesn't quite fit.

41. **Treat yourself in other ways than with food**. New candles or skincare, or a book to read if you enjoy reading. A hand craft project, or filing and painting your nails while you watch

television keeps your hands busy and you won't miss a snack as much. Look upon feeling great and looking healthy as the treat if you feel like you 'need' a snack.

42. **Script your day in the morning**. I have found it so helpful to spend a few minutes designing my day and writing out a loose plan. Once I close my journal I don't go back to it until the next day, but it's amazing if I read back how closely my day followed this 'idealistic' plan. Maybe it's gone into my subconscious, but however it works, it's a great way to stay focused on what I want to do, and do it in a lovely way as well.

43. **Commit to not complaining and not gossiping**. Negativity kills the romance vibes not only in a partnership but in your own mind. Whenever I find myself slipping in this direction, I recommit and start to feel more positive straight away. Complaining and gossiping is definitely low-vibe; looking at the bright side of things feels much better.

44. **Journal on 'My Romanticized Lifestyle'** with soft music playing and a beverage by your side. As you make notes, use this filter for how you might dress, things you'll enjoy doing, the kinds of food and drink you will choose, and how your home would ideally look. Create a

romanticized daily plan based on a workday, play day, or holiday. Dream up ways in which you can infuse your everyday with pleasant, dreamy touches.

45. **Enjoy your favourite things** *by only owning your favourite things*. It's that simple! In each category clean up your enjoyment by asking yourself if you really love owning that item. Maybe it does something useful, or it's beautiful, as William Morris says. Feel free to pass on anything that's 'only there because it's there'.

46. **You become what you practice**, so practice looking at the bright side of life, choosing beauty wherever you can, and being someone who delights in self-care and has a vibrant energy. Today I will practice feeling light in my spirit. What about you?

47. **Turn the camera on yourself** so you can see how others see you. Does your outside match how you see yourself on the inside? Work on both aspects at the same time – dress and groom as your ideal self would, and buoy up your mindset as well.

48. **Participate in life**. Be open to opportunities around you and also listen for your own wisdom. Follow the breadcrumbs that are shown to you. What this looks like for me is to

complete what I need to do on my computer and then get up out of the chair and do things!

49. **Spend time in your happy place**. Whatever activities bring you joy, do more of them. Baking, gardening, taking beautiful photos, spending time with others, taking alone time; identify what those activities are for you (and maybe even find some new ones) and indulge in them often.

50. **Romance yourself** by taking *you* out on dates, doing things *you* enjoy, and generally treating yourself like your own best friend. I love going window-shopping by myself, trying on a new perfume, browsing the bookstore, and seeing what the new fashions are. I don't do it every week, but I really enjoy it when I do take a couple of hours to stroll around town.

As you can see, romanticizing your life is a mindset shift and an accumulation of small, inexpensive or free ways to make your days a little lovelier. Sure, there will be days when you are busy, tired or grumpy (often all three go together for me) and the last thing on your mind will be creating romance for yourself.

On those days it's probably more about survival, but even then you can make things a little nicer. Treat yourself with kid gloves and take extra care when you need it the most.

It's my belief and experience that the more we treat ourselves well and endeavour to make our everyday life delightful, the rarer those off days are. When we befriend ourselves and treat 'us' nicely by making everything as pleasing as we can is when we feel like we are living our most charmed life.

Every day is a new start and a fresh opportunity to create a beautiful life for ourselves. Something I've started doing is lying in bed for a few more minutes saying positive affirmations to myself before I get up each morning.

I am ready for my fabulous day
I live a wonderful life
I love my life!
Goodness is drawn to me
Miracles will be happening today

I just dream up some new ones each day and it's incredible how they help me bounce out of bed ready to create another beautiful day in the life of Fiona.

Create your own pep talk each morning and love your life even more than you already do. Be your own cheerleader; at least there will be one person in your corner when you feel like you're on your own!

Whatever we focus on is brought to us. If we wake up feeling negative or afraid, our day unfolds thus because that's all we'll notice. But if we purposely steer our focus towards the good, we will head in that direction instead.

I have proved it to myself more times than I can count, so if you haven't done it yourself yet, please borrow my faith.

Here's to your wondrous life. Live well my friend!

To Finish

Thank you so much for reading *100 Ways to live a Soft, Calm Life*.

I sincerely hope you have gained inspiration from these pages as well as encouragement to enjoy a beautifully relaxing, peaceful, and more feminine life.

I write my books because I want to share my enthusiasm for making the most of the everyday without necessarily spending a lot of money. And to ~~brainwash~~ inspire you to do the same! To be a positive thinker and all-round happy person in spite of the risk of others making fun of you. And if someone calls you a flossy air-head to take it as a compliment!

Not everyone needs to be like us. But we get to be who we enjoy being: ladies who enjoy the little things, notice delightful touches, and don't mind even the monotonous tasks because we have made things lovely in our mind.

If you have a moment, I would be beyond grateful if you could leave me a review on Amazon. Even a few words are perfect – you don't have to write a lot. A review is the best compliment you can give to an author. It helps others find my books, and I'd love to spread my message of living well through an inspired mindset.

If you have a friend who you think would enjoy this book, please tell them about it, or loan them your copy if you bought the paperback.

And did you know that most libraries welcome suggestions on what to purchase? Maybe you might like to suggest this book for your local public library. That way, lots more people can read it!

If you have anything you'd like to say to me personally, please feel free to write:

fiona@howtobechic.com

Maybe you have a book idea for me, want to let me know what you thought of *this* book, or have even spotted an error. I hope not, but if you do find a typo, please let me know!

Think of me as your friend all the way down in New Zealand, cheering you on and wishing you well. You get to choose how good it can get, how wonderful your daily experience will be, how happy you can let yourself feel, and the fabulous heights that your relationship with yourself and others can reach.

With all my best to you, and I look forward to seeing you in my next book!

Fiona

About the Author

Fiona Ferris lives in the beautiful and sunny wine region of Hawke's Bay, New Zealand, with her husband, Paul, their rescue cat Nina, rescue dogs Daphne and Chloe, and their cousin Micky dog.

She loves to write about living a fabulous life, chic self-development and cultivating a feminine personal style. Fiona is passionate about the topic of living well, in particular that a simple and beautiful life can be achieved without spending a lot of money.

Her books are published in five languages currently: English, Spanish, Russian, Lithuanian and Vietnamese. She also runs an online home study program for aspiring non-fiction authors.

To learn more about Fiona, you can connect with her at:
howtobechic.com
fionaferris.com
facebook.com/fionaferrisauthor
twitter.com/fiona_ferris
instagram.com/fionaferrisnz
youtube.com/fionaferris

Fiona's other books are listed on the next page, and you can also find them at:
amazon.com/author/fionaferris

Other books by Fiona Ferris

Thirty Chic Days: *Practical inspiration for a beautiful life*

Thirty More Chic Days: *Creating an inspired mindset for a magical life*

Thirty Chic Days Vol. 3: *Nurturing a happy relationship, staying youthful, being your best self, and having a ton of fun at the same time*

Thirty Slim Days: *Create your slender and healthy life in a fun and enjoyable way*

Financially Chic: *Live a luxurious life on a budget, learn to love managing money, and grow your wealth*

How to be Chic in the Winter: *Living slim, happy and stylish during the cold season*

How to be Chic in the Summer: *Living well, keeping your cool and dressing stylishly when it's warm outside*

A Chic and Simple Christmas: *Celebrate the holiday season with ease and grace*

The Original 30 Chic Days Blog Series: *Be inspired by the online series that started it all*

30 Chic Days at Home: *Self-care tips for when you have to stay at home, or any other time when life is challenging*

30 Chic Days at Home Vol. 2: *Creating a serene spa-like ambience in your home for soothing peace and relaxation*

The Chic Author: *Create your dream career and lifestyle, writing and self-publishing non-fiction books*

The Chic Closet: *Inspired ideas to develop your personal style, fall in love with your wardrobe, and bring back the joy in dressing yourself*

The Peaceful Life: *Slowing down, choosing happiness, nurturing your feminine self, and finding sanctuary in your home*

Loving Your Epic Small Life: *Thriving in your own style, being happy at home, and the art of exquisite self-care*

The Glam Life: *Uplevel everything in a fun way using glamour as your filter to the world*

100 Ways *to Live a Luxurious Life on a Budget*

100 Ways *to Declutter Your Home*

100 Ways *to Live a European Inspired Life*

100 Ways *to Enjoy Self-Care for Gentle Wellbeing and a Healthy Body Image*

100 Ways *to be That Girl*

100 Ways *to Be a Chic Success and Create Your Dream Life*

Go to amazon.com/author/fionaferris to see books released since this edition was published.

Made in the USA
Columbia, SC
11 July 2024

38470563R00062